There are a few big differences between house cats and wild or big cats.

One is big cats have round eyes; house cats have slits for their pupils.

The biggest difference is in size wild cats are much larger than house cats.

Lastly, house cats have been bred to live inside with humans; wild cats need to live in the wild where they can hunt.

My First Book about the Alphabet of Big Cats

Amazing Animal Books
Children's Picture Books

By Molly Davidson

Mendon Cottage Books

JD-Biz Publishing

Read More Amazing Animal Books

Purchase at Amazon.com

Download Free Books!
http://MendonCottageBooks.com

 **is for an Asiatic Golden Cat.**

Iain Thompson © <u>Wikimedia Commons</u>

Asiatic golden cats live in Southeast Asia.

They hunt by themselves; usually birds, rabbits, rodents, goats, reptiles, and sometimes water buffalo calves.

 **is for a Bobcat.**

Bobcats are the most plentiful of all the big cats in North America.

They're in all habitats forests, swamps, deserts, and even towns; but are rarely seen because they are nocturnal, which means active at night.

B is also for a Black-Footed Cat.

Patrick Ch. Apfeld © <u>Wikimedia Commons</u>

Black-footed cats are the smallest wild cats living in Africa.

They weigh 5 pounds, live in burrows during the day, and only come out at night to hunt.

C is for a Cheetah.

Cheetahs are the World's fastest land mammal, running up to 70 miles per hour.

They can cover up to 26 feet in one stride!

They are the only big cat that does not roar, they purr instead.

C is also for a Cougar.

Cougars are also called mountain lions, panthers, pumas, and catamounts.

They live in the southern half of Canada, all over the United States, and down to the tip of South America.

They're the second heaviest cat weighing up to 210 pounds.

 **is for an Eurasian Lynx.**

Eurasian lynx live in the mountains of Central and southeast Europe.

They are the largest of the lynx species; the boys weigh up to 66 pounds and the girls weighs about 46 pounds.

F is for a Flat-Headed Cat.

Jim Sanderson © <u>Wikimedia Commons</u>

Flat-Headed Cats are endangered and are only found in Borneo, Sumatra, and on the Thai-Malay Peninsula.

They live by themselves and usually fish for food at night.

G is for Geoffroy's Cat.

Geoffroy's cats live in the mountains of southwest South America.

They get their name from a zooloigist, Etienne Geoffroy Saint-Hilaire, who discovered them on the banks of the Rio Negro in Patagonia in the 1820's.

 **is for a Homotherium.**

Apotea © Wikimedia Commons

Homotherium is a sub species of the saber-toothed tiger.

They lived for over 5 million years, but became extinct about 1 1/2 million years ago in Africa.

I is for an Iberian Lynx.

Iberian lynx are endangered and can only be found on the Iberian Peninsula in Europe.

Mother lynx give birth to 2 or 3 kittens usually in March or April.

J is for a Jaguar.

The name jaguar came from a Native American word meaning "he who kills with one leap."

Two million year old fossils have been found of jaguars.

They are the largest cats living in South America; they weigh up to 250 pounds.

 **is for a Kodkod.**

Jim Sanderson © Wikimedia Commons

Kodkods are the smallest cats found in the western hemisphere, they live in the forests of Chile and Argentina.

They are the same size as a house cat and are active during the day and the night.

L is for a Lion.

An adult lion's roar can be heard up to 5 miles away!

Lions are the only big cat to live in groups, they are called a pride.

They are also the only big cat to have a tuft of hair at the end of their tail.

L is also for a Leopard.

Leopards are the strongest of the big cats; they can carry prey twice their weight up a tree.

Mother leopards give birth usually to two cubs, which are gray with light spots, they live with her until they learn to hunt; around 2 years.

 **is for a Mountain Lion.**

Mountain lions have the largest range of any mammal, besides a human, in the Western Hemisphere.

They are excellent jumpers, because they have strong muscular back legs that are longer than their front legs.

N is for a Neofelis Nebulosa, the scientific name for a Clouded Leopard.

Clouded leopards are an endangered big cat found in the rainforests of Indonesia.

They have rotating ankles which help them climb down trees head first, extremely fast.

 **is for an Ocelot.**

Ocelots can be found hunting monkeys and other animals at night in the rainforests of South America.

They have rough tongues which help to clean every bit of meat off the bones of their prey.

P is for a Panther.

Panthers are also called black cougars, black leopards, and black jaguars depending on where you are in the World.

Baby cubs learn to hunt as young as 2 to 3 months old.

P is also for a Pallas Cat.

Pallas cats' fur changes color depending on the season; they are grey in the winter and reddish in the summer.

They are active during the early morning and late afternoon, they sleep in caves during the middle of the day.

They have the longest fur of any cat.

 is for a Rusty-Spotted Cat.

UrLunkwill © <u>Wikimedia Commons</u>

Rusty-spotted cats are two times smaller than house cats; they live the forest and mountains of India and Sri Lanka.

S is for a Snow Leopard.

Snow leopards have long, muscular back legs which allow them to leap 7 times their body length in one leap.

They are rare and endangered living in the mountains of central Asia.

S is also for a Serval.

Servals have the largest ears, in comparison to their body, of any cat.

They catch 50% of all the animals they hunt; most cats only catch 10%.

They can run up to 50 miles per hour; only the cheetah is faster than them.

T is for a Tiger.

Every tiger has their own stripe pattern, no two are alike.

Tigers are the largest of the big cats, weighing up to 500 pounds, and are excellent swimmers.

They live about 8 - 10 years in the wild.

 **is for a Wildcat.**

Wildcats are excellent climbers, but do most of their hunting on the ground, at night.

X is for a Xenosmilus.

Jared © Wikimedia Commons

Xenosmilus is an extinct big cat; scientists believe they weighed up to 880 pounds!

They were very muscular and were members of the saber-toothed tiger species.

Y is in the scientific name for a Jaguarondi, which is Puma Yagouaroundi.

Jaguarondis are also called otter cats, and they live in southern North America, Mexico, and South America.

They can jump over 6 feet in the air to catch a flying bird to eat.

Z is for a Zanzibar Leopard.

Peter Maas © <u>Wikimedia Commons</u>

Zanzibar leopards are very rare and may actually be extinct.

They live only on the Zanzibar archipelago in Tanzania.

Conclusion

I hope you have enjoyed reading about some amazing big cats.

One more fact, there are really just 5 main species that make up all the big cats in the World; tigers, lions, jaguars, leopards, and cheetahs, everything else is just a subspecies.

Our books are available at

1. Amazon.com

2. Barnes and Noble

3. Itunes

4. Kobo

5. Smashwords

6. Google Play Books

Download Free Books!
http://MendonCottageBooks.com

Publisher

JD-Biz Corp

P O Box 374

Mendon, Utah 84325

http://www.jd-biz.com/